Lilith

LEA MALOT

For Hugo

Contents

Inside The Outsider
Annecy
The S Word
The Apple Tree
The Time
St Mary's
Men
February Friends
Harry
Monsters
Marina
Migraine
Montceau Les Mines
Mirrors
Whitstable
Papa
Matt
It Was You
Birthday Girl
The Rich People
Joe
Matt, Again
The Heavy Ladies
Moonlit Boy
Skin And Bones
Lilith
Plates On Sticks
Letters
The Lovers
Wedding Day
To My Future Lover
July
I Am

LILITH

Inside The Outsider

Do they see me, do they feel what I feel?
Is their heart broken, are they truly feeling connected?
Are their ugly, bitten nails showing what's underneath?
Can somebody get me out of here?

Poor girl, lost in a sea of faces
Grinning and pretending to know her way
I scream and scream and scream- the whole world can hear me
She used to be so kind but all they did was twist her mind

Sit up straight, smile, know when to stop talking
Don't show what's inside, they don't want to hear
What's that ring? Will you tell me its story?
Who are those people? Have I lost all sense of belonging?

I am small woman and my soul feels trapped
A loser, a bum, the outsider
I put on a show when they're around- ladies and gentlemen, won't you look at me!
Lying is an art, like everything else, and I am incredible at it

I am a cloud drifting by, a stray on the roam
Where to go? Where's my home?
The outside is fun, I'm a fucking wild card
The inside is deep and lonely, and much too dark

Sitting on the outside behind this glass window
Those people who think they know
I'm the wrong damn girl in the wrong damn room
I go on my own again, and I know I'll be asked why I left so soon.

Annecy

This is the lake I've grown by, and this is me
The shades of blue have substance and frightens deeply
One toe in it— you'll sink.
The pain that lies in these waters has no mercy

My broken, sorry, empty being arises from the bottom- all the gods' hands haul me through the relentless and icy wind
How many times have I lost myself in the sunsets glittering over the gentle tide
This is the cauldron, this is the place where you dive and die.

There is a sunken ship— we all know this is the place of resting for the bloody bodies who had the same mind and heart that I do
The surface is a thin veil between two worlds— a hospital for souls and the land of the fools.
The minutes are years here, and the great escape is something similar to tons of piled fantasies
Animals in cages in the nunnery, non religious, yet every move is watched by entities.

I bleed, he stares— punishes and wounds me.
In this place, only the toughest will win
I was born out of thin air they like to call love
I was raised by adults in deathmasks and a forced marriage that felt like screams of agony.

Were they friends or were they enemies? They hissed. How to know
When I'm still getting bandaged from their knives in my heart from years ago
When their laughter sounded like the depths of sorrow
When their words felt like salt on my cuts, like a tentacle pulling me under, the soft water getting all the way to my core

It's over now.

The S Word

Their eyes are red like clean and sharp rubies. Is it
That they're inspecting me? Seeing through me? Do they know
All of what I've done, the crimes I've been commiting
My sinful being. My marriage with the devil.

A forced touch that feels rough like dry moss
Horrifying thing next to me— I turn and I toss
My mind winds to my God
But I don't call him, I don't call him at all.

And I float, I rise so high, I'm wonderfully light— I might myself just be a God.
A mean one, an obnoxious and horrible entity, but one nonetheless
Creatures and animals want to gnaw at my flesh
They crave me, my eyes, my arms, my skin, my bones.

The night isn't mine. It slips out of my sight like a lizard's tail
One moment it was there, then the beast found me
On the edge, and the moon is watching. It sees me in hell
There's a fire that's been set. The awful and dirty four walls close on my body

I'm scared and I ring the bell, the bell, the bell.
It's dead, empty as an abandoned cocoon. Dry and cracking
I think I died— how boring is it, what a way to go.
I open my eyes and I stretch my bloody limbs— I never went at all.

A door slams and resonates through my soul
I'm not complete, the beast took something from me.
It won't give it back, and left without a word. A freak
I'm painted black now.

The Apple Tree

One minute it was there, then it vanished.
I almost touched it, felt it grazing my bloody fingertips
The nightly creature chose to leave me, you, my friends and enemies
A big, fat, gold present that was denied from me

I know the beast, I know what it does
I know its qualities, its secrets, its flaws
Buzzing like a bee. It tires me.
I've been waiting, static, for too long— under this apple tree

If you only knew how the days are killing my soul
They are dragging, pulling me under, beneath the ugly stones
Under this black veil, it's hiding me
Here— here is my safe place. I can pretend I don't exist.

Let me go, please won't you let me go, let something go
Let go of my timeless eyes, my shimmery skin
Forgetfulness. It is bliss.
In the morning it will be different— wait until tomorrow

I can disappear like a bird in the sky
It's not that hard for me as it is for you.
I can click my fingers and let the cold death choose
Does it want me, does it want my body, how hard do I have to try

And the world is melting like everything in the summer
What a thrill— this is cinematic, click, click, click, enigmatic
Filthy minds. You are happiness borrowers
I'm better off in this place, your voices can't get through, I sit still.

The Time

And there it comes— the feeling you thought you'd forgotten
Loneliness feels stifling, cold, rough. It is an invisible force. It holds me down
Like an invisible tornado is pushing me into my dusty mattress, down, harder
Nobody sees the force except for me, and I let myself drown

Being the underdog is overrated, believe me
It's being too much all the while not being enough.
And the whole sea is inside of me, it's seething, raging, its dissatisfactions resonating through my being
I'm tired, weary, exhausted and cannot bear to stay in my home

I feel like a shadow but the worst possible kind. I'm not haunting and important, I am ignored. How to be special?
And the darkness that used to be my friend now wants me to die
And I run, I scream, I fly, it's not time. It's not my time.

I might have cried enough to create a new ocean.
I might have done enough for men to love me.
I might have laughed enough to make them feel important.
I might have made enough mistakes for them to flee.

St Mary's

I heard a voice calling me.
A distorted one, frightening, dusty and full of risks, but a voice nonetheless.
My vision split
I heard the chilly Gods and their deathless deaths

There was a line to cross, white as clean snow, pure like a virgin's tears
And compelled to it, foolish and young, I walked across it
My two legs took me where I never was supposed to be
At a time when deceased souls come out of their rotten, grey skin.

Oh my— what a thrill!
They're inviting me. I feel a sense of belonging.
No bones, no dislocated jaws, no foul smell of flesh— this is nothing like it
The ghouls are putting on a big show for me. They are dancing and stomping.

And they want me to stay, stay, stay, stay.
Their voices resonate through my ears like loud rusty bells
Among the ghosts, I have found a home.
The asphalt is suddenly quicksand under my naked toes

Stop holding onto my hair, I have to go now.
Stop hurting me, or I won't come back tomorrow.
Violence has never been the answer to this, you know.
Let me go, let me go, let me go.

Men

Armies of the foul decay within human race
It's a war— me against them
Silence, my song.

My wedding gown, the grace of silk and pearls
I want to burn it. It does not belong on cruel planet Earth.
His laugh sounds like a mockingbird's. I want it to sound like the depths of
goodness, but it is utterly distasteful

And every moment tastes of disaster
My love flows freely in the rivers for strangers to sink in, and the crowd
approaches to suck my tears
I am bruised and battered. I'm a corpse.

Men, you lure me into obscurity.
I fear and dread the dark cells your words lock me in
Your gender was made without a heart. God is to blame.

February Friends

You, right there— it appears you caught my eye
It seems you stick out of the ugly and dull crowd
What are you? What are you, I wonder

If your soul is cold, or warm like the summer
Are you one of those dreamers? Or do you get through life
Like I wish I could, wish I could, wish I could.

I know you now— yes, I do.
You're the opposite of a sin, nothing like an awful dream
Face like a statue. Clean and pure as a baby.

If the moon was human, it would resemble you
You leave the same impression of something overwhelmingly beautiful
But mysterious— with a dark side, black eyes, lonely, searching, reaching.

Mouth the shape of a kiss
I question if within you is any magic
You shine, you catch on fire, you disappear.

I am terrified by this dark thing that is in men
It bites, it screams, it gets a hold of them.
There is no guile or warp in you, and my arms wrap themselves around you
tight, tight, tightly.

And the dark cloud that hovers over my being fears you.
It knows that you don't see it, and that in your eyes it isn't true
You believe in me, and you push it away, away, away

It is fine, all is good now, I wait.
Until the pale sun rises, over my body
And I am on my own. I soak in every beam.

Harry

One magpie for I don't want this anymore,
Two magpies for please walk out the door,
Three magpies for I'm leaving you on your own,
Four magpies for nothing can save our love.

The dry paint on this masterpiece hung on my heart crackles and flakes off
I drew it carefully, slowly, beautifully, artistically, but it never made anything any better
One glance at it and you can only see the pain, the shed tears and dried blood
I look at it and see nothing less than beauty, attachment, salt skin and fire.

And that song that we sang those sweaty and rosy nights of August
It is gone, gone, gone.
My passion and my undying love for you meant nothing but danger
Boiling, seething, exploding— and now it's turned into grey ash, ugly dust and ice cold snow.

In the bed that we burnt and fell for each other a bit harder, a bit harder, a bit harder in those long summer nights
I saw myself blooming like a flower when it was finally time, like a fragile butterfly
I can't stop wondering why I see you at night and you're gouging your dark eyes out
I believe the sight of me is something you would rather never have to deal with again, now.

I reach for your hand at the end of my bed while you're holding onto the new girl
Eyes the colour of sunny spring skies and her hair all the shades of summer
My ebony locks, tired eyes and gloomy appearance can't live up to what God has given her
I had to let you go, watch you replace me while I screamed, kicked, wept and you made it look like nothing for you had ever been easier

For every misspoken word or sight that you don't want to see,
There is a charge, a very big charge from you—
For my broken heart and constant stifling nostalgy for the memories that steal the air from me,
Nothing you will do, do, do.

Writing, crying, what an easy thing to do when you're sitting on your own in bed,
I know you can tell I'm not fully, entirely through
And I'm aware that while you're trying to wish me away,
I still hold onto the souvenirs my mind still has from you.

Monsters

Now now, who will be next on the list?
Who will take my soul and turn it to dust?
You, right there. Would you like to torture me?
Don't worry— after a while, it doesn't hurt

Dangerous creatures, they roam free
Their costumes, their nodding, their charming game
Ugly souls, made of sand, moss and rotten bouquets of lilies
Empty as awful seashells.

Their brains work like golden machines
Incredibly fast but devoid of real identity
Who are they? What do they do? And what do they want from me?
One, then another. They pass through me like ghosts with no sense of belonging

My body is an ocean to them, to their curious eyes
They leave it unexplored, selfish and lazy sailors
For their need to play with it, swim in it, admire its curves and waves, there is a charge
For keeping it close and understanding its abyss— it really goes.

It's coming closer, and I keep a steady breath, I clench my fists
The creature will not smell my fear, my fear, my fear.
I know how it goes, dear friend, dearest enemy
Now, I am your valuable— your golden doll, quiet and shiny

My bones hold the stillness of my sorrow
You do not know what I am
One of those black-feathered birds. A crow
I cannot turn into a pure swan again

Back to the start, or arrived at the end
Machine, creature, animal, are you terrified?
Left me alone, a corpse. Your claws tore apart and took my thoughts, my soul and my breath
Everything else was too much or never enough.

Marina

The sun rises over her sleeping body— it is spectacular
It reaches the inside of every curve, every crook, every fold of every sheet
This is what it feels like to feel complete. To stare at something so luminous and bright
Her white flesh reflects the beams, the heat, the light

Birds fly in the horizon. They will remember us.
Feelings vague as fog, but it is love, love, love
Friendship never sounded real until I met you, until I heard your laugh
The waves crashing on the shore— making you happy. I found my call.

Millions of fishes in the sea, but you are the one I have chosen
Shiny scales, silver and blue, and life in your eyes
Flawless like a clean slate. Nothing like the others
They're terrible! Lifeless, clueless, I don't want that, no, I don't want that.

And the sky and the clouds glitters over the ocean. A labour of love
And the sea is everything but steady, like everything inside me
Moving, shaking, jiggling— I can feel my heart beating
No word is pretty enough to register the intensity of my feelings, of everything about you and me

How you envelop me in your innocent arms and listen
Quietly, you listen, listen, listen, listen. And for you only I still fight
When the dark cloud comes upon me, I think of your huge, blue eyes in those lights
And forget. About everything else. It is gone and obliterated.

Migraine

I have to pretend I feel real
Like the sky above me isn't falling
Act like the world isn't melting
Not weep and learn to keep it in

That's the way they like you
Unproblematic, wonderful, easy to talk to
So they can connect
Isn't that the only way?

And the boy sitting at the edge of my bed
He doesn't know, and doesn't want to
Isn't willing to help to roll away that constant headache
The kind that feels like your skull is being filled with rusty screws

Stay quiet and maybe they will accept your presence
Because with your mouth shut, you are silver, gold, even
A living doll they can admire, for an instant
Like a magic, shining witch who escaped the coven

What about the man who will marry me?
Will his love be enough to dissolve my sorrow and my bad dreams?
I'll be wearing my prettiest dress, I can guarantee
White and lacy, believe me, they'll bury me in it

Like the cat, I have nine times to die
But isn't once enough?
There has been one time, then another time, then another time
Try again, six more chances for you to close your eyes and finally shut

This life is a theatre number
I annihilate each act and character
I give them what they want to see
The big strip tease, gentlemen, ladies

Then suddenly I have turned to nothing
You poke, you stir, empty, just an amber ring
I've burnt down but I rise out of the ashes, I scream
I'm the phoenix, with my dark hair, are you now feeling what I feel?

Montceau Les Mines

This town means danger.
It is evergreen, yet pinching at my soul, an awfully jagged and ripped poster
It is inhabited by a billion cries that I can hear when I put myself to sleep
Where is my smile? Where is my soul? Where is my greatness? Disappeared.

In this great masterpiece I am hidden behind the hellish fires
The flames are licking at my flesh prison tenderly and lovingly
When they see me, the burning souls are gouging their eyes out.
The sight of pureness is poison to them. Now, I can see it.

I never knew how to love those with whom I share a bloodline.
Their words and touch were nothing else than empty, empty, full of this ugly emptiness
Not the peaceful kind— the one that makes you weary and broken inside
The one that leaves you asking why. It is in their eyes, in their smiles, in their faces.

I was a child
You couldn't forgive me because it was always <u>harder</u>
I was only a child
With a loaded gun for a father.

And the ghost of the past creeps up under my sheets and my skin when the dark night falls.
Its invisible hand chokes me when a lover's voice gets louder
The minute I see a hand being raised it pulls me under
Leaves at dawn

Mirrors

What an oddity— tonight the mirror talked to me.
I was brushing and brushing and brushing my hair until I stopped thinking
A voice. Clear as ice. A bald cry.
Safety is gone after your sudden and startling arrival.

You ask, you question, you pinch at my brain
And you can reach for it, you know how to, stupid thing.
The forest-like maze that is my mind has become your playground
How is it in there, empty? Or full of insecurities and answers I never found.

I am naked as a baby— a fat baby, I think. Not the beautiful kind.
Do you care? You're teasing. Do you mind. Do you love yourself. Do you?
Are you satisfied? Do you care, please tell me, do you. Does it feel right?
You keep questioning until I spit out the words. I do.

Winter melancholy has taken its toll on me
It opens a window that I wish I could close effortlessly.
The wind comes through with your words and your ghoulish songs
My self-assurance flakes off. It's like Christmas when the snow falls from the sky. I'm slowly dissolving into something that's not me, something that you own.

I can't dance. I'm not enough to dance.
Neither can I smile— I lost it somewhere. It is irretrievable.
Some days I'm like a cow, others I feel like a bird. Most days you're trapped in a bell jar, seldom you break out and find your way to my left shoulder.
It is my best side.

Whitstable

The low tide washes over the neat pebbles. It covers their bald surface
This is the sea, quiet, in all its impressive and godly greatness

Immensity. He is holding tight onto my hand
Today, I feel— pain is not present. I fondly enjoy its absence

And the clouds over us feel like they could collapse and break the scenery
What a waste would it be, I think. I have two legs and I walk until I'm aching

The fishermen are out and see the tourists. I can hear their hisses of distress
And suddenly, without a warning, something inside me clicks. It's wrong.

The sharp air fills my lungs. It feels cold but somehow aphrodisiac
Maybe I used to be a creature of the sea. I am fascinated by every sound

And the colourful houses that look like sheds are planted right here, like flowers
One, then another, then another— I lost count after a dozen.

Today, I am a smile. I am filled with pride and I am a sun beam.
How divine, you have no idea how divine. People smile with those teeth that look like polished pearls. Everybody is beautiful— it's not the ugliness of the city

If you knew what I would give for the water to swallow me whole
For the salt to shape me into something more beautiful, special, bold.

This is what it feels like to be complete. This is childhood number two
I tell my lover I never knew that, I never knew it could happen to somebody like me. My childhood was unfairly cruel.

The crabs, stupid animals. They try to pinch at the palm of my hand
I suddenly throw it back in the water. It wants to go home.

Time is ticking and silently, I say a prayer for it to stop. I have found where I belong.
But God doesn't listen— the traitor.

He knows I called him that. He banished me from the sea
I haven't seen it since.

Papa

Papa, you passed it onto me. We are fools
Didn't get your blue eyes or your humour
Or your love for white lies and strong, awful booze
I got your mind— and your black soul

We have this in common, I know, know, know
You have been flickering for as long as I've lived
On, off, on, off, on, then off.
I have always felt abandoned like a dirty accident, an atrocious and ugly baby

Papa, you are as immense and dark as the sky, but heavier.
Clouds falling onto me, onto them, onto her— there is nothing you will do
You are grey, glaucous and cold like the gloomy winter
And every man I see has something that's yours.

I have always been scared of you,
With your hard language and your voice breaking through the roof
But you're smooth, you know when not to hurt
That does not make you any less of the devil.

I was sixteen when you broke my pretty red heart in two
And you never wanted to accept that you, out of all of them, would be the one to
How many times have I tried to die to get away from you
I thought even the bones would do.

Papa, I think I've had enough
You made room for me in your fat, scarred heart, but I'm through
You lure me back in— wait for me to get close and weak because of your insane love
I've seen too much of you, I'm telling you. Papa, I'm through.

Matt

I shall never forget the emotions crawling up into my skin and bones when I first laid my eyes on you.
The old anarchy of my sorrows disappeared for a night or two.

Hampstead was our place, out of all of them.
Historical streets and May sunsets. For a mere moment, nothing was worth fearing— not even the merciless darkness

The Heath will always remind me of the sound of your voice
It is the only one I will never let go of.

The mute sky looking over us, and I felt nothing less than celestial
You felt it too— our walls collapsed, tumbled down. Nakedness. Between you and I.

They have you, they keep you stuck and encased in some sort of glossy pellicle.
I could never win against it. It felt indestructible.

I fought against the waves that kept pulling you in. Our shadows touched and made love under the palest of moonlights.
That mouth made to do violence on, over and over. You had me, you had me, you had me.

My dreams were never worth much— but they came true with every hollow breath you stole I was ignited. I became whole.
The city that has you is my sworn enemy, for it killed what could have been.

I let you step in the dustiest corners no one had ever seen. You cherished it, gave it some sort of worship.
Daylight is gone, as you are. I'll wait. It is no trouble.

It Was You

He gives you a chance. Do not take it, for it is poisonous and oozing with bad intentions
The second you get a taste of what could be, it slips out of your sight and there again, I faced my old friend abandon
My tongue feels like fire and I spit out the flames, but I am the fool. I boil in the sin-filled cauldron.

All my life I've been so lonely, no home sweet and no sweet home
When his touch makes me feel like I belong- the moment the villain becomes my very own God
Reaches out for my heart, but there is emptiness. Emptiness, and the neverending gaping hole.

I undress my mind before his hungry eyes- he sees all of me. The pretty and the ugly.
He says I am fascinating and that my eyes sparkle, and that for who I am, I should never be sorry
Selfish soul. Undeserving.

How laughable- after all, I've had my go with happiness, no more chances for me
I don't want the rose with the poisonous thorn. The sting couldn't even make me feel a thing.
Sitting in silence and getting used to the numbness is what I do best, at least I know exactly the way to do it

And I miss every man who's ever wanted to see through me, even the ones who could never feel what I feel
For before they lost me, they had me
I was art to them, but I imagine you would someday have had enough of the greatest masterpiece

Shine a light on me
I'm here
I'm here.

(

Birthday Girl

The pain is malicious. It has had me locked me in the darkest of rooms for quite some time now.
The suffering has scorched me to the very root
I am a handful of wires, crimson coloured filaments flying around.

I have broken and put myself together enough to know it never lasts
I must have lost count of how many sunsets and sunrises have passed.
I cannot tolerate any more. I am a shriek that gets lost— always too loud or not enough.

I must have cried enough to create a new ocean— I carry its waves, its dissatisfactions deep within me
I move with every wave, with every hurricane, with every tsunami
It harms me. But it won't kill, it won't kill, it won't kill.

The door has opened. I thought the light would finally be drawn to my pale and dark being
Utterly unasked for, the beast stepped in heavily and found its way inside of me.
The eyes of a sort of wild predator, mouthful of blood, claws, and the way they felt, the way they scarred me, I can't stop thinking of it, of it, it, it.

How the light was this nearly acidic and toxic yellow. It burnt through my skull. Floating on an invisible cloud, no reflection, he took away my name, made its way to my insides, like a dirty and worthless worm.
I don't remember who I am, nor who I was.

And now I am on my own again.
I am left in this suffocating darkness.
I miss the fire inside of my heart. I don't miss the madness. The shame, the shame, the shame.

The Rich People

Is it perfection or is it just another illusion
Is it their place or did they choose to make it belong to them ?
I feel at home where they are
I am nothing like them, they're a bore, and I am nothing less than art.

They are average birds that have become rare and earned some sort of worth
They are not Godsent, my Lord, they are quite the opposite
Saints but nobody knows their names
Mannequins. Silk, pearls, anything.

This, they claimed. It is theirs. Do not touch it.
And theywordlessly frown upon us like we're walking catastrophes
We might be, we might just be.
Sat under weeping willow trees, we act like we're part of the silent cult. But still in touch with the sad reality.

They don't know love, they know beach houses, fur coats, and ugliness.
They know their golden watches and the way to execute a perfect handshake
We know demons, they say it's madness
We know real, and they know fake.

Joe

What I love is the eyes, the eyes, the eyes
Struck me like lightning, Joe.
Baby-faced, wearing the darkest of black
You secretly always had me, Joe.

Your laugh could echo all the way up through the atmosphere and reach the milky stars
It rises, it rises, it rises.
My own face is flushed and warm. I see right through you, I think I do
Never in my mere existence have I ever seen a sky so blue.

My ideas and thoughts shimmer— every single word counts
How we would like to believe in anything, Joe.
There is something between us and the ugly, boring rich people with their crooked teeth and fake smiles
Clouds are flowering, and I feel alive, Joe.

The sun has seen us— it has seen every single impure thought we have
There is no punishment. There is only light
I breathe in the invisibles and the glittering oxygen reaches everything within me
I feel lighter than anything.

A door is opened before us. Do not go there
It might ruin every good and pure thing we feel, Joe.
It is blindly shiny and painfully reachable— it wants us. It wants to cast the spell
I'm never going to walk through it if you don't, Joe.

Before my eyes, the world has turned into some sort of mirror-like, shiny haze
It is empty— how awfully empty.
There is you and there is me. I resist the urge to sabotage it
Pure like ice, and nothing less.

Matt, Again

An hour of introspective stasis
In the forgotten corners of my mind, in the smallest and most narrow breaches, there is you.
Child-like, jumping up and down, participating in a one-player game of hide and seek
A side of my lover that I never knew

I look around the crowded and obscure room
There is no joy. There is only that awful, ghastly pretending
Ghosts of souls that have surrendered— they are dancing and stomping on the reflection of the moon
I don't feel at peace. I feel sorry.

I dragged and walked the weight of my sorrows home by my side
Half of them won't stop talking about you
For such sad things, they're too excitable. They eat all of my oxygen. I quite almost died.
I would have rathered shut down than to be laying here, being tortured because of what I can't undo

I love you— but I will never say it out loud
My heart is red like a poppy and beating like a tambourine the second I think of your face that one night
I rue the day I dared to kiss you back in the dark— I didn't think. I have you locked the most blissful corner of my mind
I'll love you until the trees change in the fall, and beyond that. I will love you until it fades. Until my heart finds a way to be without you, Matt.

The Heavy Ladies

The faceless voices of my childhood were quieter today
They might have begun to accept me as I am.
There was the incessant fight, the salty tears, the encased ideas of the monster I was not supposed to be
I let them down. I let them down badly.

Insanity is being talked about. Cow-like ladies whose husband left years ago.
Want to tell me how to act, how to dress, how to be the person they want me to be
Give me advice, ring the bell, tell me places to go
Don't eat this, don't carry yourself that way, be thin, be quiet and be pretty.

They have lost. I've had enough.
Long nights of wondering. Life sucked out of me, I was drained to the very last drop
The heavy ladies wanted to drink my soul in wine glasses, sneering at who I was
Shame on them ! Look at what I've become.

The voices can't get through.
The line they used is broken.
Can't touch who I am now, a woman in a shining armour.
I am alive. I breathe. I have a chance, too.

Moonlit Boy

It's been three short weeks, my heart told me.
The moon says it might have been six. Exactly fourty-two days since our hearts collided under its cold and fluorescent light.

Summer love, infatuation that smelled of wine and berries
I can't have a glass without having to taste you on my lips.

Maybe I held onto you too tight, my love, I know I might have
And maybe all you wanted was to go and run off into something else, fearless as a bird in flight.

The chain linking both of our souls has been broken.
A few are to blame- me, playing the wrong cards, and the words you carelessly left unspoken.

My heart a glass balloon, shattered.
Cut me, cut me, cut me. The bastard.

Skin And Bones

In the mirror, I stare. There is nothing.
Not a soul inside this body I seem to not inhabit.
I lift my eyes to the sky and let go of the disappointment and hurt
This is a battle. One to be won.

There have been too many of them, now, I'm exhausted.
I want to lie in the grass staring at the night. It is infinitely bigger than I am
A war that left me scarred, oh so scarred
The lies, the lies, the lies.

I am sick to death of the feeling of sorrow
It won't let me go
I am a goddess. But I resemble something much less celestial
The pain will never leave me alone.

There must be some zip, a button. I could slide out of this ever-so-dreaded skin
Be a skeleton, ghostly presence, that walks, that breathes, that talks
Not like a doll. A thing so much more impossible to be
My dreams of me are loud and filled with smoke

For all it matters, I am alive.

Lilith

On your shoulder sits what could have been
Our child. We named her Lilith.
Called her the name of the Goddess of pain and fear
Sadness was something that would always have us wrapped around its finger, for eternity

You're laughing, straight from the heart. It sounds like a song.
You never went away. You stayed, and we held each other until the sun rose
The love inside of us was raging
And today, my love, I feel it.

I had a dream, a silly dream
That the city that had you would hand you back, back, back to me.
Like a present, with a glossy ribbon and confetti
I'll always be wasting away, waiting.

I see us by the sea. Surrounded by the frightening infinity.
The first time I saw you, we were stuck between the ghosts and trees
There is everything and nothing. We won't break up in pieces that fly around like dust
We will stand still, for there is you, there is me, and there is us.

We forgot about the heartbreak. It filled us up like poison.
I wish I could say the same about both of our still present demons
On your shoulder, you have it, my love. You have it all.
I annihilate each memory of when you left and never came home.

Plates On Sticks

If spinning plates on sticks was an art, believe me, I would be quite the entertainer
I have done it ever since I can remember, since I can feel, since I can suffer
How many times have I felt consumed by the neverending frenzy of it and the hurt
One of them falls, and the whole of me crumbles

I have seen enough of them loudly shatter on the hard floor and I have lost something each time
Crimson colour, you are my wrath— onyx-like, you are my dreams
Mustard, boredom. Mint green, serenity.
Each of them holds and contains what I am

I want to sleep, to rest, I am exhausted
Every year and every season is eating me alive
I shut my eyes and the world turns red
Letting go feels like stepping on my own in something much bigger than I am and much more hostile

I am sorry to those I've loved and who have had to endlessly keep on spinning the plates
Called me a liability.
Said I always found a way to put something that could've been to waste
Those puppets could not bear the weight of me

There is no stillness within me, only a raging and violent storm
I search for some sense of stability in everyone who dares to cross my path or look into my eyes
One day I might learn. I am better on my own.
The only place I can lose myself into is with the girl I love, in the warmth of my very own arms.

Letters

The first letter was sent on a stormy September evening
My bones cracked as the walls watched me. The depths of my soul were far darker than the icy, onyx-like night sky.
I am the furthest thing from an insomniac, and this I will promise
I seldom lay awake after dusk. Purely to try and get past the memories and the innocent child-like cries.

The second letter was not long after, most certainly must have been in that same amber-coloured Autumn
This entourage of mine turned into air-like figures. Mannequins— their voices poured inside of me.
I'm not asleep— but still, I beg to wake up
The hurt is as big as death. It stays, it giggles, its cold center appears almost sweet.

I've lost count of how many letters I wrote when the immaculate snow was falling down on the bare and gone nature
It might have been ten, it might have been twenty. Endless, how painfully endless.
The new year rolled in with its heavy steps and hopes higher than the clouds. I had imagined another sort of allure.
Walked through the door, snuck under my sheets. Said it could make me golden and better.

I gave all to them. I became as empty as my heart
Took the knives and carved me like a pumpkin. Split me in half, still stiff and alive.
Death and its unforgiving eyes. Beautiful, how breathtaking it was. How unreachable.
But like every thing I crave, it wasn't given at all. My letters were delivered— but I have to give it time.

I am haunted by a scream that inhabitates the deepest corners of my mind.
Every fold of my skin holds it hostage, like a prisoner.
Considers me an idle. It's almost Stockholm syndrome. It could flee— it could fly
But it stays. It stays, it stays. It might just be there for ever.

The Lovers

Red is the colour of me.
It is blood, it is poppies, it is pain, it is passion
White is the colour of him
It is serenity, it is smoke, it is purity, it is the snow.

If I was a bird, I would be a crow.
If he was one also, he would be a dove
How could one love the other, this, I don't think I will ever know
I could attempt to understand and one day, I shall.

He joins me and helps painting the night a darker colour
I accompany him. Make the world somehow brighter.
I am Lilith, I am the Queen of Darkness
You are not afraid. You are brave and know this love is worth seeing my own Hell.

All your life you've loved anything crisp and precise
Your life is a moon-sized clock, ticking regularly, a little too fast.
It is not like mine, no, it is not like mine
Chaos, black thoughts, the emotional clutter and the lies

I know the bottom and I do not fear it anymore, for I have been there
All you've ever known was shallow.
I used to be alone. I don't want this anymore, I dream of the great escape.
And you understand, understand, understand. Won't let go.

Remember when you moved in me
Every wall shook, the immensity of the earthquake going through my body
You felt it too. You were shaking
That's when I knew you meant it.

Wedding Day

Welcome, this day is cold, this day is hard, this day feels much too official
The stern and cold vibe of a funeral
Serious words and forced grins that they call smiles
Is it what forever love is all about ?

Loving so much that it would be considered a passion crime
Hard as a rock, painful as heartbreak, possessed by something that's never been quite alive
I stared at the old stone church walls for as long as I could
I couldn't make out the fire in their hearts, I saw it all, but nothing worth crying over like you really should.

Is that love then- a dull and easy declaration
In front of hungry cameras and curious, demonic eyes. Nothing genuine.
I expected words that could cause earthquakes, I expected tears, I expected the most burning passion
If it is what real love is, I do not want it.

I might be too young and wild to see it.
And maybe this sort of watered down infatuation is everything I'll never be
I might be a fool, the most ignorant in this land. I didn't know love could be freeing
That it does not have to be burning, breaking, suffering.

Wedding days. Fake, fake, faking.
Cloudly skies. Sun is away
Your eyes are not smiling.
It will show on photographs. You will rue the day.

To My Future Lover

It's stood on my chest– stiff like a stick head to toe, holding me down like some sort of heavy stone
The need, the need, the need.
I am young and free as a sunbeam and can afford to be waiting– it doesn't believe so
Won't give me peace at night, another lost shriek

Every full moon I water myself down slightly more. I wonder how much there is left of who I truly am.
The thought alone is killing my days.
I breathe in and wonder if that's the weight of me nobody could possibly bear
And if in order to feel that odd yet vital marvel, I must kill of me what I can

My heart and its fiery love is beating hard, hard, hard for no one, no body, no touch, no brain.
No face I can admire and dream of in my darkest hours
I would take the numb parts in my lover and put it amongst the flames to revive what they thought they'd never feel again
I would do it quietly, carefully, with the purest intentions and no hurt.

I dream of choosing you, stranger, in every lifetime I'll be allowed to live and suffer through
I wish to let go of the birds stuck in my ribcage– daring to call themselves love.
They want to come out, sneakily but gently make their way inside of you.
An angel whose skin would taste of the sweetest liquor, who will come and someday be gone
And even then, future lover, I will swim like a mermaid through the Earth and the soil to rest next to your bones.

I am ready for it, to be utterly and unquestionably loveable
Put aside my fears, my demons, my words and my mask.
Death is overrated anyway. I'm not as impressed as I used to be with her anymore.

There are no lies now, there is the wait, the wait, the wait, and you. You, who every part of my being will adore.

July

In this place, I never stop learning
Peacefulness, vast, yet empty.
Who I was, I don't know.
Here, I am whoever I choose to be

I am being watched, but I am getting used to the feeling
Histrionic tendencies are being satisfied, or so it appears
They see me as a smile. Here, I am no storm, no explosion. Nothing.
Swabbed clear of the chaos. I can finally breathe.

The air is calm, there is plenty
No more of the suffocating feeling in my sore and fiery throat
My lungs are filled with the green of the fields, the utopic scenery
Happiness ever so subtle. A change that might not last long.

I am sick of the baggage I carry everywhere I go
Papa, Papa. It's all your fault.
I am pure as morning dew and you are thunder
Last week, Papa. I saw you. You made my heart break more than I knew it
could ever be shattered.

Somebody must have made you cold, who was it, Papa ?
I think about it and it destroys me. Some questions will never be answered.
Words better left unspoken, Papa
I've learned how to be on my own without you, far away from the crimes you
commited.

The walls are white and motionless. I know them.
I know the history, I know they love me
The eyes, the mouths, the bloodless deaths
I love them back. For eternity.

I Am

I am the relentless waves crashing with violence on the rocky shore
The minute I return from my Roman Holiday in Hell and your arms feel like home

I am the ocean you could never tame- my substanceless blue-black infinity that overwhelms
When you, curious sailor, with the tears I've crystallised on your child-like face, peek at the inside of my being, of my soul, of my idle brain.

I am the tongue of the dead
I speak of beginnings, but of no ends.

I am dried blood on porcelain skin
When I wake of my nightly fight with the devil, that stole yet again something from me

I am God's cherished Goddess
Before your eyes, I undress

I am every hurricane, I am the rage, I am power and nothing less
I am woman, I am chaos, I am the violence in the pouring rain and the soul of a burning flame